The Four Faces of Eve

About this Book:

Intimate. Honest. Personal. Universal. I love the premise of this book. Four women. Four voices joined in a single expression that opens again and again, all of the poems exploring what it is to be a woman who loves, who aches, who is beaten down and rises up. Four voices interweaving to explore the great spectrum of what it is to be alive.

Reading this collection, I can feel the connection between the four poets—how the trust they developed over years of writing together has fostered courage, authenticity, vulnerability and great strength. To slip into the pages of *The Four Faces of Eve* is like listening to four parts singing together in a choir—alone, they might be lovely, but together, they bring a richness that takes the breath away, then gives it back.

    Rosemerry Wahtola Trommer, author of *The Unfolding*
    and host of *The Poetic Path*

The Four Faces of Eve is an ambitious project in ... [six] parts by four poets that moves through the experiences of speakers who identify as women in relationships with partners, family, and their own belief systems.

These poems vary widely in terms of form and content but what shines through is the feeling of a legacy of survival that starts with these women and runs off the page to millions of women before now and millions to come. From the sensory details of their environments ("if it is really cold/ smells of coffee blow in") to desire ("our skin grows/ eyes") to death and grief ("not the sympathetic   oh..../ the   oh no"), this collection feels like a mirror shattered on the pavement, reflecting memories and eyes and hands and bellies and toes of different types of women facing myriad violence and myriad joy and continuing to catch the light.

    Carla Sofia Ferreira, 2024 Faulkner-Wisdom Competition Judge
    (*The Four Faces of Eve* manuscript was First Runner-Up for Poetry)

The powerfully intimate poems in *The Four Faces of Eve* transport us to another time and place where experiences of love, loss, deep despair, and high hope can be illuminated. What an incredible gift to us! Be prepared to laugh and cry, to discover and savor personal insights as each heartfelt story is devoured.

        Nancy Saltzman, author of *Radical Survivor: One Woman's Path Through Life, Love, and Uncharted Tragedy*

In *The Four Faces of Eve*, the powerful, braided voices of Boyle, Granville, Perkins, and Waldstein sound out strong and affirming. Often playful and possessed of good humor, these poems do not shy from the pain, loss, and joys that shape lives and sustain art. How fortunate that these poets found each other and how lucky for us to have this book in the world.

        Aaron Anstett, author most recently of *Late-Stage Everything* and *What Now*

Boyle, Perkins, Granville, and Waldstein, all in their 70s and 80s — pull no punches as they explore the myriad dimensions of their lives. As members of their self-named Mad Women's Poetry Society for many years, they have mastered the art of supporting each other through the trials and tribulations they've faced not only as mature women but as writers plumbing the depths of their often-devastating life experiences in their very personal and powerful poetry.

Each of these poets is not only prolific but widely published, and their diverse personal and professional backgrounds contribute to the varied insights they provide. While painful universal themes such as abuse, betrayal, and loss are explored ... the four poets offer unique takes and insights on those themes, making this multidimensional collection all the more compelling. And despite their despair at times, they also infuse many of their poems with the joy they've experienced as women in love, women as mothers, women as their own persons armed with what they need to not only survive ... but to flourish as artists.

Often set in locales that resonate, from Puget Sound to Jones Beach, or in the homes of "Jersey Nana" or "Oklahoma Grandma" (Boyle 32), these poems are peppered with memorable images of larkspurs and cardinals; log cabins and pottery; familiar celestial objects as well as nature made celestial. Floating and even walking on water, flights and migrations, fears and refractions, regrets and remembrances are woven through *The Four Faces of Eve* alongside rings of truth as well as joy over what once was, and wistfulness over what might have been. Resilience, ownership, self-preservation, and pride sit side by side with the unmentionables not only mentioned but declared for all to see and hear. The power of desire and the upending of ecstasy, selves lost in moments of delight as much as in moments of unmooring...all this is trumpeted unabashedly despite what "polite" society so often insists women — and especially women of a certain age — should keep to themselves.

        Karen DeGroot Carter, author of *One Sister's Song* and *Not Nearly Everything You Need to Know about Writing*

The Four Faces of Eve

by

Constance E. Boyle

Brooke Granville

Petra Perkins

Gail Waldstein

Golden Antelope Press
715 E. McPherson
Kirksville, Missouri 63501
2025

Copyright ©2025 by Constance E. Boyle, Brooke Granville, Petra Perkins and Gail Waldstein. (Each author retains copyright for her individual poems.)

Cover Design by Russell Nelson

Interior Drawings by M7Studio, Abdul TubaDesign, Tuhin Prodesign, AbraSa, SeVector, and Olga Krupenikova

Author Photo Credit: Katy Tartakoff, for Constance Boyle and Gail Waldstein

All rights reserved. No portion of this publication may be duplicated in any way without the expressed written consent of the publisher, except in the form of brief excerpts or quotations for review purposes.

ISBN   978-1-952232-93-0

Library of Congress Control Number: 2024950828

Published by:
Golden Antelope Press
715 E. McPherson
Kirksville, Missouri 63501

Available at:
Golden Antelope Press
715 E. McPherson
Kirksville, Missouri, 63501
Phone: (660) 229-2997
http://www.goldenantelope.com
Email: ndelmoni@gmail.com

We Want to Thank

Elizabeth Haukaas for creating our critique group in 1998, and to gratefully acknowledge poets Hildegard Guttendorfer, Joy Stross, Margaret Walther and Hilary DePolo as vital members of our group through the years.

Contents

Introductions   1

#WeToo   5
    Daddy / *Gail Waldstein* 6
    helium / *Gail Waldstein* 7
    hymn / *Gail Waldstein* 8
    The Interview / *Petra Perkins* 9
    Listing / *Petra Perkins* 10
    stoop / *Constance E. Boyle* 12
    attic / *Constance E. Boyle* 13
    in-house / *Constance E. Boyle* 14
    early first marriage / *Brooke Granville* 15
    black and blue / *Brooke Granville* 16
    betrayal / *Brooke Granville* 17
    last betrayal / *Brooke Granville* 18

Amour   19
    Chili in Winter / *Petra Perkins* 20
    Summer's Fall / *Petra Perkins* 22
    The Kiss / *Petra Perkins* 24
    Driveway / *Petra Perkins* 26
    kayaking in a two-person boat / *Constance E. Boyle* 27
    dance 101 / *Constance E. Boyle* 28
    I Didn't Know / *Constance E. Boyle* 30
    styling / *Constance E. Boyle* 32
    things I wished I'd saved / *Brooke Granville* 33
    interloper / *Brooke Granville* 34
    your vessel / *Brooke Granville* 35
    vacuum / *Brooke Granville* 36
    afterwards / *Brooke Granville* 37
    Aunt Kay mugs / *Brooke Granville* 38

first kiss / *Gail Waldstein* 39
a duet of novices / *Gail Waldstein* 40
through meadows and marriages / *Gail Waldstein* 41
chasm / *Gail Waldstein* 42

Motherhood 43
A Covid Mother's Day / *Petra Perkins* 44
migration / *Brooke Granville* 46
expression / *Brooke Granville* 47
no room / *Brooke Granville* 48
in Big Sky / *Brooke Granville* 49
new year's eve '88 / *Brooke Granville* 50
passage / *Constance E. Boyle* 51
colt / *Constance E. Boyle* 52
mom, you'll love this / *Constance E. Boyle* 53
gravity slack belly / *Gail Waldstein* 54
womb-dreams / *Gail Waldstein* 55
grief canal / *Gail Waldstein* 56
and the sins / *Gail Waldstein* 57
a vase of lonely / *Gail Waldstein* 58

Resilience 59
I'll tell you bipolar / *Constance E. Boyle* 60
bipolar II / *Constance E. Boyle* 61
the sun's claim / *Constance E. Boyle* 62
this time of Covid-19 / *Constance E. Boyle* 63
East River moon / *Gail Waldstein* 66
In the Closet / *Petra Perkins* 68
my son's chair / *Brooke Granville* 71

Death/Grief 73
missing / *Brooke Granville* 74
the oh of suicide / *Brooke Granville* 75
I didn't dust for a decade / *Brooke Granville* 76
grief is nocturnal / *Brooke Granville* 77
listening for the dead / *Brooke Granville* 78
prayer for the light baby / *Gail Waldstein* 79
water baby / *Gail Waldstein* 81
second cancer / *Gail Waldstein* 82
rapid / *Gail Waldstein* 83
two thousand miles / *Constance E. Boyle* 87
a hike to a waterfall in Ithaca four weeks after / *Constance E. Boyle* . 88
Five Weeks / *Petra Perkins* 90

CONTENTS

Here and Away / *Petra Perkins* 91
Heat / *Petra Perkins* 92
Retreating / *Petra Perkins* 96
Grief Takes No Prisoners / *Petra Perkins* 97

Spirit   **101**
aurora / *Gail Waldstein* 102
flying / *Constance E. Boyle* 106
Beehive mountain / *Brooke Granville* 108
Waxing Crescent / *Petra Perkins* 109
Celestial / *Petra Perkins* 110
Through the Pane / *Petra Perkins* 113

Credits and Acknowledgments   **117**

Introductions

We, the self-named *Mad Woman's Poetry Society*, Constance E. Boyle, Brooke Granville, Petra Perkins and Gail Waldstein, are four women living in Colorado. We have individual voices, different passions, points of view, causes, and styles. As mature women, each of us possesses a treasure of experiences and accumulated wisdom, both painful and pleasurable, gained from a rich, full, 70-80 years of living. Coming from diverse backgrounds with varied careers and work histories, we hold precious the joy of being in each other's lives, sharing, and affecting each other's ways of seeing.

Our poetry collection, *The Four Faces of Eve*, showcases familiar elements of life from multiple angles and dimensions. Recognizing that experiences overlap, and that threads are intricately interwoven, we name our six themes: (1) #WeToo; (2) Amour; (3) Motherhood; (4) Resilience; (5) Death and Grief; and (6) Spirit. Each of us is represented by at least one poem in each of the collection's thematic sections. (Forewarning: some of the poems are of a sensitive nature, with depictions of abuse, suicide, and other subjects.)

We chose the name *Eve* because it is derived from definitions of *life* and *to live, to give life,* and *to breathe*. Eve, in our context, is all of that and more. We breathe—sometimes quietly, sometimes not. We live with love; we give life and appreciate the gift; we hold on to the strength that living requires; we deal with breath's final passing; and we celebrate life's spirit.

We're also connecting our collective work with a classic film, *The Three Faces of Eve*. In the movie, a woman with "multiple personality disorder" manifests as three different personas, each dealing with assumptions about how a woman should act. In the film, there's a resolution into an integrated third persona. Our book, *The Four Faces of Eve* recognizes how deeply we experience and empathize with each other's work.

Each of us has experienced being dismissed as too emotional or being ignored or discounted because we are female or "only the wife." Or now, because we are senior. We have also been blessed by knowing the unbalanced pull of desire, the mad rush of love, the disabling torpor of grief, and the incredible happiness of being a mother. To try and define our perspectives, two images from theater come to mind– the paired masks of laughter and sorrow. Yet there are many subtler divisions of emotions: serenity, sexual passion, curiosity, stinging humor, boredom, anger, disgust, terror. The list is long.

Thus, our #WeToo section addresses several types of abuse: sexual, emotional and physical, occurring at different stages of life and involving discrepant relationships between perpetrator and victim. Our *Amour* selections are intimate and eclectic recollections of the exuberance, awe, and heartbreak of love, whether it's love between romantic partners or that of a parent for a child.

Motherhood defines us, becomes part of our identity as it weaves throughout our relationships as mothers/stepmothers/adoptive mothers, as grandmothers, and as daughters, molding us into better humans. Despite the difficulties we sometimes encounter, we're rewarded with incredible love and (almost) never-ending hopefulness.

In *Resilience*, we share our challenges with mental health and the aftermaths of disease or trauma, whether our own of those of others. Our overall theme in *The Four Faces of Eve* is one of resilient survival. Still, in our fifth section, *Death/Grief*, you'll find a deep well into which each of us has fallen, a well in which we have experienced dissolution, known how it feels to be breathless, lost. Our final section, *Spirit* celebrates hope, gratitude, and joy, the magical something which happens when life breathes peace and energy into us.

In *The Four Faces of Eve*, we offer you 73 discrete yet connected and overlapping texts. We offer close-up exposure to a multitude of faces, caught as they react to the storms, droughts, and occasional sunshowers of life. We work through poetry, through nuanced verse, through conjured image, through the power of the written word.

A little about our collaboration, and then about ourselves

Our bi-monthly poetry critiques begin with catching up and tuning in to each other. Our process is then to read aloud each poem (which we've sent out beforehand), listening for its music and its mood. We move from poet to poet. The author reads her poem and then each listener offers suggestions for improving it. These can include word substitutions, further attention to sounds, rhythms, titles, reordering of parts, deletions of images (or occasionally of whole poems) which don't resonate, and brainstorming additions—the sort which might bubble up when four trusted friends delve more deeply into a story's world. We are:

Constance E. Boyle (Connie) worked as a physician assistant in pediatric and adolescent medicine. She is married with three children and four grandchildren. Writing *Curious George* sequels at age six initiated her writing life. Her poems in this collection reflect moments in her personal life, and include snapshots of motherhood (*passage, colt* and *Mom, you'll love this*), of her own experiences with childhood trauma (*stoop, attic,* and *in-house*) and with bipolar illness (*I'll tell you bipolar, bipolar II,* and *the sun's claim*), and a visit to her daughters in New York City (*flying*).

Connie's stylistic approach is to use space to convey breath and breaks, with minimal punctuation and capitalization. Marjory Wentworth, judge for the 2014 Faulkner-Wisdom Competition said about *flying*: *"The poem is in three sections; each begins with a word and its definition, paired with a short prose poem describing a moment in a particular woman's life. The definitions are unique, incorporating breath spaces ... suggesting the use of erasure. [They become] litanies [on] the words "white" and "flying," ... expand[ing] our ideas about the words in a meditative way. The sweep of this poem is dazzling.*

Before **Brooke Granville** was five years old, she had been a part of three families. Her birth mother relinquished her to a couple who had buried two sons a few months earlier. Their trauma and grief were more than a baby daughter could fix, and they divorced. Her adoptive parents each remarried within a year. Brooke and her mother's new husband (a recent widower) and his eight-year-old daughter moved into a red brick Tudor. This house meant stability for her new family. The concept of home, so important to Brooke, led her to a four-decade career in residential real estate.

During her brief early marriage, while mothering two young children, Brooke leaned on poetry to express herself. She has continued to write– through divorce, her son's suicide, a second marriage and another child. She connected with her birth family in her 60s. Over twenty years ago, Brooke joined Connie Boyle and Gail Waldstein in a critique group which Petra Perkins later became part of. This book, recording their collective experience of womanhood, is the result.

Petra Perkins began writing poetry as a child and never stopped. It was originally a way to make her dad laugh, but later, after his early sudden death, poetry became a solace, as it later was with the sudden accidental deaths of her husband and older son ("Here and Away") and later with the devastating illness of her daughter ("A Covid Mother's Day"). After her aerospace career ended, Petra became a full-time writer of memoir, fiction, poetry, and essay.

She reads or writes poetry before tackling other genres, to "warm up the imagery juices." Petra often employs dialogue in her poems and enjoys playing with experimental hybrid and prose formats ("Through the Pane" and "The Kiss"). Her process for writing a poem is rarely pre-planned; poetry comes out in streams of consciousness. "Chili in Winter" and "Waxing Crescent" exemplify this pattern, and further illustrate Petra's humorous and sensuous vision of Eve.

Gail Waldstein, Brooklyn born, moved to Jersey as a child. She escaped an abusive father and went to college and medical school on full scholarships. Freshman year of med school, she fell madly in love with an upperclassman and married. They had three children during her internship and training. The family worked well until it didn't. Divorced, she raised three precious kids alone for fifteen chaotic, happy years. During her 37-year pediatric-pathology practice, she diagnosed tumors, leukemias and malformations in babies and children, did an overwhelming number of autopsies, worked in genetics, thrived. She remarried (another failed adventure), then survived two serious cancers, the latter, life-threatening.

Gail began creative writing in the nineties. When poetry arrived, stealing breath, demanding attention, it stopped all other activity (except tending emergencies), insisted words be recorded. Her poems relate powerful personal events, joy, beauty, sorrow. When spirit boils in her, she writes. Grateful for every day, every awesome child, treasured grandchild, each word-gift....

#WeToo

Daddy

maybe it doesn't
matter   what you did
or didn't do

what I remember   or was it
false   a kind of
neuronal   scrabble

tiles in a game, say
scan the board   weigh letters
produce high numbers: win

your fall jacket   chalk coated
you demanded top grades
from me   always   hundreds

a measure of
not who I was
or how I felt

when you felt me

you slammed the basement door   all
went black   you whispered   *be quiet*
of course it doesn't hurt   *Daddy would never*

do I recall this   was that
possible   a child's mind is
mauve   her secret

an aging brain   twirls, insecure
memories   flash purple like pain
what matters now is   what do I do
                       with what's left

                          ~Gail Waldstein

helium

my father's   bedside

his breathing stops   starts
lips parched with the labor
of biting air

he clasps my hand
ferocious grasp
pulls me to him

outside   palm fronds   slap
pink adobe walls
a small window   curtains rain

balloons bracket us   get well

he's sullen since his stroke
tugs my hand   like a stutter
in   and   in

one last command
                stroke me

                        ~*Gail Waldstein*

hymn

Behold, I stand at the door and knock. Rev. 3:20

safe after years of
        you   stalking me
        now   in a new hall
        outside my door

you   plead
        can I come in
        my tongue   dries
        pebbled-mute

maybe you're not at the door
        our marriage wasn't   that brutal
        all this is nothing   but
                a hallucination

still   you stand there
        pity is   history's rubble
        how does the voice say   *no*
        knowing this particular   refusal

        may be this body's final
                chance of intimacy

~Gail Waldstein

The Interview

I hired him because of his looks, something men often did
given the choice between a drop-dead gorgeous woman or
a smart plain one. Oh, yeah six-six, I guesstimated,
gazing up at this tower of testosterone. I offered him a chair
across from me – nothing between us – his legs went on
forever, stretched like a street you might like to walk down.

Hands, parked on his slim knees in spider pose: up down
up down. Ginormous feet, sleek in handmade Italian loafers.
I imagined Michelangelo's *David* with shoes pretty spendy,
trendy, for a young engineer whose package was nothing if
not stunning with Tom Selleck dimple & Harrison Ford hair.

I don't remember asking him difficult questions as
was my usual style in weeding out candidates. Time passed
like lightning. I couldn't get past the sparky meteoric eyes
flashing me, flashing at me, flirtatiously (or so I imagined).

Dark bushy eyebrows, distracting! He expertly maneuvered
them: up down up down. How I wanted to get in there and
prune them.

His exit trail had a fresh lingering lime-y scent of aftershave.
I realized I'd never offered him a job. *See you Monday then?*
he'd said quick as his wink, gliding away, not missing a beat.

He'd led me to a grandstand like I was the drum major of his
one-woman band, my baton conducting a young man's march
up the corporate ladder: up up up, until he rose to the level of
his incompetence.

~Petra Perkins

Listing

He said he had 42 reasons   exactly   why he left her
He'd written them on a list   on his first night alone
    Do you want to read it? he asked
        pulling a folded sheet from his wallet
        passing it across the bar

He'd waited   until the kids were out of college
        until his wife of 25 years
        high school sweetheart
        was gone for the day

He packed   worked fast from a list…
suitcases/ bags/ clothes/ books/ small furniture/
guitar/ his mother's watercolors/ shot-glass collection/
tools/ grandfather's WWII trunk he'd never opened /
guns/ DVD porn collection/ family photos (none of her)
/ Christmas stocking/ chopped firewood/
                          …carried the items to a trailer
                hooked to his Trailblazer
        made a vodka tonic
sat on the patio   a redwood deck he'd built
                                    waiting

When she drove in   right on time
    he read another list   then handed it to her
Getting a divorce/ No more counseling/ You took
    me for granted/ Lawyer will call tomorrow
    / I never loved you

He jumped into the truck   before the stunned woman
    (mother of their beloved children)
    could utter one single word

He gunned   the accelerator   hauled ass
    and since the path from the house is gravelly dirt
    there was a cloud of dust
He looked in the rearview mirror but couldn't see her

He told me this story and more   over a bottle of wine
    I could see her   standing there as he zooms away
    I could feel her   body and brain in shock
    I could taste the bile in her throat

No, I don't want to read it.

                                        ~Petra Perkins

stoop

if it is really cold
smells of coffee blow in
from a factory the next town over

wind hints
rain   whips skirts up
bottoms freeze
either place   steps or landing
                                  grow
numb the longer I sit
cotton underthings don't keep
cold from cutting flesh until

bones become part stone
even when I'm not locked
out I sit on cold

slabs   going in is giving in   giving in
                          to other things

I prefer cold

~Constance E. Boyle

attic

afternoons I sneak to the attic   pass
my parents' closet

squeeze through the mid-sized
opening   dodge hangers crammed

with shirts   hide traces of me

heat encases the attic
no breeze   breathless

the hotter   the purer
        I do penance
like nuns in the convent

down the street   kneel on wood floors
repeat Hail Marys   flog and atone

unfinished planks smell freshly cut
floorboards creak underfoot   the only

noise in my private space   I sit on old boxes
perch on an edge   sweat trickles

I see movement   turn   see nothing

a silverfish darts across the floor
it stops   ashy gray feelers in front

two raised hairs   immobile as that insect—
me on my bed   unbreathing

waiting for my father to sleep   hoping
he won't   rise up   exposed   knowing

he will   I wait until he starts toward me   then
leave   the best way I can

~Constance E. Boyle

in-house

Nana's Victrola sits on a wide table
opera solos from the large brass horn
Sunday morning visits   I finger
the listening dog on the wood base, careful
not to jar the arm from its groove   watch
the needle   inch toward center

at the dining table   a starched cloth
we eat éclairs   cream thick, sweet
on our lips   summer /winter   the house
always warm   robust soprano Maria Callas
stirs my small chest   her trill splits
the air   Nana's table   unlike the one
at home

    Saturday mornings   Dad
removes the lace cloth   leans over me
I lie   still   no air   no breath
        no song

~Constance E. Boyle

early first marriage

pregnant   married at twenty
tried to be grown ups

moved into your
grandma Twyla's basement

you worked as a TV salesman
across town

within a year
my father gave you a job

you confided one night
while we were in bed

I'm in love
      with the secretary at work

we haven't done it yet
      so I'm doing the right thing here
           letting you know

you rolled over and went to sleep

I tried to make you hard   one last time

                      ~Brooke Granville

black   and blue

Front door slams open
He grabs my arms
Holds me against the wall
My feet dangle
He spits   *you've been whoring around*
i whisper
i love you baby   you know that
i've been right here   waiting
i fixed your dinner   let me get it for you
He loosens his grip   pushes me against the doorjamb
i crumple to the floor   go to the kitchen
Next day   hanging diapers on the clothesline
He throws a long sleeve shirt at me
Put this on   nobody wants to see your bruises

~Brooke Granville

betrayal

our two-year-old daughter
cries for you
especially   nap   bedtime

how to explain
    daddy
        is with the secretary now

close her door   to our whimpers

wander the sparse walk-up
        hopelessness   in hand

~Brooke Granville

last betrayal

baby on my hip   keys in hand
     our old station wagon
parked on the street

     driver's side headlight
         front panel   bashed in

husband still sleeping
    I rush in to tell him
       rouses

     slurs
oh yeah   *I thought I might*
have hit something last night
on my way home from the bar

           ~Brooke Granville

Amour

Chili in Winter

Students of carnal knowledge need a break now and then,
share a meal, besides, we'd wearied reciting Great Books
weekends in bed and bath, my lusty illicit professor of English
Lit'rature, canned-cream-of-bland-mushroom-soup hotdish maker, he,
I, naïve high priestess of the frozen lean cuisine,
slide the banister, *au naturel*, to kitchen, to his declaration:
"Today we raise slothful asses, do some *rrreal* cookin',"
*rrr*eeling me in, I say, "O-*kay*, good lookin', heat this place up,
whence he ropes my Godiva hair (*Will we* ever *eat*?) "Make haste,"
I urge, "my appetite's tameless on just a hunka hunka burnin' love!"
steeped by foreplay... a skinny-dip into *Remembrance of Things Past*
(blissfully unaware that Proust can change lives),
Mr. Rochester's lulling "chase dull care away," in *Jane Eyre*,
Lady Chatterley's Lover (utter rapture!) and Papa Hemingway's lust...
our catalyst turns out to be the unforeseen and silly, pork green chili,
igniting record heights of ardor this afternoon (*ahem*, impossible
given our smug certainty we'd already invented Nirvana
as we strained life's expectancy of mattress springs)
alluring me, his inner child of New Mexico where chili is legion/religion,
my heart swells, seeing his secret ingredients, worries unfounded
re his hints of idolizing macho Papa (who shot his own safari banquets)
– a literary infatuation! – now a sensitivity unleashes,
slips an apron over neck, draping breasts, slow-kissing each,
is this pre-marital bliss we're testing, or a chili recipe? Holy Toledo,
(that's where *I'm* from, btw, where love is rarified, food not sanctified)
I am impressed   OMG aroused *again*
we slice, measure, weigh, braise...
our union erases frost on blinds; icicles on window ledges drop dead;
smoke seeps from us smo-oh-oh-ldering
on old, scorched countertops, but we, young and fresh,
can't help it, burning itsy bitsy booboos on our tooshies, ahh,
dudes... much panting occurs *avant* seeding, dicing, boiling
those lewd Big Jim roasted peppers,
(y'know, Bobby Flay would be proud) we are hot human chipotles,
libidos sparring on front burners, we park seasonings on rear,
chop hard little jalapenos, onions, rolled in sugar,
he points, "Plant your sublime smackeroo here, ohhh *ye-ah*, sweet Jesus
Halleluiah, keep that pork greased and glistening, add dabs of garlic,
cumin (sounds nice), cilantro, celery salt, oregano, cinnamon spice,
let s*immer*, gl*immer*..." (weeping, begging) "lick my tongue, *Yi*,
Yi, you *taste* like New Mexico *smells*, woman, feed my famished passion,

ahh, Epicurean delight... savor our succulent feast..."
"Whoa!" I slap his drool and salty tears, "Yo, Dr. XXX, I'm over the moon,
I'm burning up on re-entry; I'm either dying or taking you home!"
my old desire to linger in the sweet spot, gone, those warm beds with
Marcel sipping tea and eating madeleines, gone
now that I'm taught to cook and dance and savor and prance, yes, I'm
hooked, your kitchen capers will ever inspire this shiver I'm in,
so yes, I'll marry you, and not because we're possibly two hours pregnant"
fingers too lethal, stained w/chili juice, to don the condom.

~Petra Perkins

Summer's Fall

my hair up
so hot outside   he

looks at me   differently
behind his Ray-Bans

he slides them off
attention lingers

there
my naked neck

surely   I blush
maybe   I bloom

he cradles my head
in one hand   coolly

slow-petting my
nape wet tendrils

caresses   each strand
making whispery wafts

then over   to the place
bottom lower earlobe

gently   gentlemanly
with the curve of

his little finger
as a blind man   might

decide   about beauty
one stroke at a time

power of touch
attuned   he seduces

skin   cells   nerves
neck   ear   heart

maybe   two minutes
no more than five

I fall   into Forever
a soft landing

~Petra Perkins

The Kiss

Cloudy Puget Sound: on a pier's last stand
      they stood alone, over pillowed whitecaps,
She and He, awaiting an approaching ferry,
      I thought as much, perhaps.

   Strolling water's edge under weepy willows
      I stopped to honor the sublime pose,
an embracing kiss of passion, misty seaside beauty
      for I had some lunchtime to lose.

   Though my gaze found livelier places to linger
      it kept returning to their private fervor
which, after minutes (five) became a public work of art
      - a traveler's monument - "Kissing Goodbye"
... however, one can tire of admiring, say, a Picasso
      or even a Michelangelo, you know,
and, who knows how it flows with protracted partings
      which start with good intentions but dampen
with inherent sadness, regrets, rarely ending in gladness
      yet their long kiss did not submit to any of those
or to any pause whatsoever; to mop their brows or lips,
      instead moving ever tighter, if they moved at all,
pressed deeper into each other as the ship's bow inched closer,
      a tall, single silhouette in raincoats
          as they lengthened into ultimate longing,
            and though you may (I did) surmise it a death
      - which is intrusion if spied on - I could not *not* watch
      for no coupling in the known history of kissing
could have locked arms, noses, legs, hair as intimately
      with the world encroaching, with the clock ticking,
nor but few kisses have likely been tendered so perfectly
      merged into a single smudge on grey sky...

   ... He/She barely breathing, you could tell
      and I, too, found my breath a whisper
hoping for a secret spell or merciful fate to intervene
      while the ferryboat ferried and passengers passed,
arrivers and leavers, running late or with leisure
      the lovers' shared eye not seeing, their ear not hearing,
me not blinking to keep them in sight
      as long as it lasted, to cast in memory the farewell

because this was a Forever Goodbye, done like none before,
    amidst crowds of oblivious travelers, failing to halt
their tracks in awe at this stunning event of legendary kissing,
    advancing loudly, *en masse*, as our statue
continued its profound, soundless bliss… these quiet lovers
    who slowed time for their monumental ceremony
where, understandably, they could not say the word "goodbye"
    you could see them not speak, so why
in this brief span called life, divide a single heart
    when they could not finalize the final act,
        could not voice one word to seal the pact?
    thus The Kiss became the word, longer than life,
and will surely endure us with no terminus, unlike most
    which are over in a lightning bolt, this one etched
eternal in annals of undying love – a timeless kiss –

    to which we come naïve but leave certain
that Shakespearians cannot imitate such gentle valediction,
    that master artists cannot conjure such exquisite emotion
so witnessed by me until my skin sparked and I exhaled,
    the boat tooting its departure inside a thunderclap
before a torrent tapped and unleashed blinding tears
    seeped with rain into weeping willow roots.

:   :   :   :   :
    :   :   :   :
   :   :   :

    You may know I was glad to miss the finale
        - his breaking away, walking the plank -
      He, the one gone, as She stood alone.
    I had her to thank.

        ~Petra Perkins

Driveway

You stand waving

your big heart at me

like the flag

above your silver head.

It is always the same

departures turned melodramas

as I pull away

to the airport

or the mere post office.

Anywhere. The grocery store.

A sendoff smile

eclipses the sun

as you fake a monkey walk

arms akimbo

or downward facing pig

one leg up

or an Irish jig.

Always something new

you do to make me laugh.

How lucky am I

knowing how lucky I am.

I want to stay

~Petra Perkins

kayaking in a two-person boat

shining water   motionless
a man and a woman press

into a kayak   neither touches

the guide advises *strongest
in the back*

the man assumes the lead
seat   kayak strays left   the man

sits   she paddles   kayak strays right
the man paddles   doesn't speak

doesn't whistle as the boat spins
backwards

which way do we go   *which way do we row*

it works best   he says   *if each rows
opposite*   the kayak crashes into

mangrove branches
the woman hits the water

with her oar   away from twisted
roots she's sure are snakes   *shout out*

a direction she says   hears *left*   they
row together

boat sails forward   centered   floating marriage

                                       ~Constance E. Boyle

dance 101

my husband, in another man's
arms   who flings him   dips
him to the floor   executing

a lovely tango   my husband takes
the lead   practices his moves
the music stops   the dance instructor

looks at me   *your turn, let's
see your stuff*
I move in   expect encircling

arms   but he pushes his palm
against mine   dances
me down the floor   moving backwards,

away from me, he brings me
forward   at the end of the room we spin
around   easy with this instructor

then it's my husband and me
on the floor   in the middle of a foxtrot
I trip over his feet

our instructor says *the man leads
a woman never leads*   he praises my
husband with no further words for me

I can't stay quiet *but I lead
naturally   I need more
signals*   the instructor tells me I need to

pick up clues my partner gives
his are too subtle, I say   *can't
a woman ever lead?*   the instructor

shakes his head   hour up   he
tells us he's leaving for upstate
New York—to help his brother
build a house   we hear nothing

more, take no further
lessons   my husband waits

for me   I wait for a teacher
who will let me lead

~Constance E. Boyle

I Didn't Know

for my aunt

how alive you were   until long after
you left   your arms

encircled our small frames   warmed us
bones sang   your laugh   infectious   included us

~

midnights   you take my sister and me
to the park   we eat Italian ice   sour   lemon

our tongues   freeze/ crave more after
the last melts in pleated cups

we wake Sunday mornings   lie quiet
in the bed shared with you   wait

for you to rise   not as early
as we want   wait

as we wait   for no one else

you feed us yogurt   a spoonful
of honey   tangy/sweet

after breakfast   we catch
the train   Jones Beach   you carry

that red cloth sack   towels poking out
boiled eggs   nectarines   salt

the train screeches in
stops   for us to board

climbs out of the tunnel   onto
a bridge   we pass

tall apartments   tenements   race
away from your New York Village flat
toward the sea   where we disembark
                        for the swim of our lives

~*Constance E. Boyle*

styling

one hundred strokes   Nana says   make
it shine   upstairs at the dressing table
we twins watch Jersey Nana
brush chin-length hair with
a pearl-handled brush— tuck pin curls
into a hairnet   sometimes
                        she brushes our hair

Oklahoma Grandma braids her hair
before the dressing table   on a quilted bench
thick plaits fall to her waist   a pewter
brush, darkened with time   she divides
each tress in thirds   twists   forms two coils
pins them   we stare in awe   never
do we see hair like this   a ritual during rare
visits   we cannot miss

they fix their hair each night   each becomes
someone else   our grandmothers   strangers
with the hair of young women   we'll never   know

~Constance E. Boyle

things I wished I'd saved

nana's mechanical bank with the bird that dropped coins into its nest
    her red Revlon nail polish she always wore

mother's wicker purse with the bamboo handles that made her
    a happier person when she carried it

my step-father's Stetson cowboy hat   light sweat stain
    around the headband he wore everywhere   but the pool

my collection of Beatles records I bought at Woolworths every time
    a new one was released

my middle child's life

        ~Brooke Granville

interloper

my father's funeral
        us   estranged   decades

his widow and son   sit front pew
        I slide into the back row

the chapel's stained-glass windows
kaleidoscope mourners

we lived in the same city
drank the same water

a father   should send birthday cards

                              ~*Brooke Granville*

your vessel

pushed out   to float
in the waters of baptism
daily mass   altar boy
parochialism anchored you

histories/stories
spoken in past tense
       as we found ourselves
in us

I came to you divorced
       moored to the
         shore of my children

now   stand on my pier
       child on each hand
belly full with your first child

ropes tighten as your boat
       familiar/familial

strains away   from my shore

I try to walk on water

~Brooke Granville

vacuum

emptiness of space; a space partially exhausted; void; a state of isolation

my ex   upgraded
thirty years ago   gave his old Hoover
to our daughter

    when they were still speaking

she bought a new vacuum
twenty years ago
passed the hand-me-down along to me

    when he and I were still speaking

today   Christmas tree
I didn't want   dragged out
pine needles scattered

       wrestle the vacuum upstairs
attachments   retractable cord
vinyl hose has split   repair with electrical tape

    will they speak when I die

~*Brooke Granville*

afterwards

your stepfather and our friends
    clear out your apartment

        the one with south windows
            crystals hanging from guitar wires

your life
    in black trash bags

music   cassettes   cd's   vinyl
    your drawings of sports cars   M. C. Escher posters

jeans and t-shirts
    hand-me-down dresser to the basement

your mattress   propped against our garage wall
    I bury my face in the scent of you

one day it is gone

        did my husband see me   arms outstretched

cheek against the blue and white ticking   muffling my sobs

        ~*Brooke Granville*

Aunt Kay mugs

she arrives
    us strangers
        sister
            of the woman who gave me away

drove a hundred miles
    gave me a pair of mugs
        thrown in her studio
            carved ovals and leaf patterns

I favor one with bold greens
    my daily coffee   nighttime tea
        palm its warmth each winter

came to visit her in Montana
    September cold front sweeping in
        she and her daughter wait for me
            in the driveway
                cupping their Aunt Kay mugs

~Brooke Granville

first kiss

explosion from a   stranger's mouth
the freshness of   new tastes
pupils expand   in each other's
mirrored eye
a new construction

test used thoughts   old selves
on   this possibility
listen rapt   to told tales
stories so staid, so often said
they have   their own rhythm

the mystery   the excitement is
this novel pulse
electricity   so crisp and vibrant
even driving past   new lovers
embracing   in a snowstorm
whips the head   pulls heart's
memory   resurrects desire

renews   visceral reactions
wets pants   sparks a fire
but   I love my current kiss

~Gail Waldstein

a duet of novices

onyx beach   opulent lava
Oregon coast
lapped by   cooling waves

stones suck soles in   curl
arches before we swim
in water so green

our skin grows   eyes
I braid my hair   raven then
as coastal pebbles   you

run with our children
their bodies supple
as fetal membranes

I see that *us*   from now
a cooling corpse
we laved the body   caress

spread a blanket   spread ourselves

the tide retreats   passion almost
pulseless   we fling our limbs
clasp each other   sunset ebbs

we gaze west   in pacific deception
as if Lazarus might
               wash ashore

~Gail Waldstein

through meadows and marriages

1. first pasture   Catskills   combed alfalfa   John petting
   pants wet   straw in black hair slick with brilliantine

2. Colorado   first husband's handsome   distraught
   she's just released from nuthouse   so mad she's quit trying
   children so small   they're barely there

3. summer drifts   fields of short Pasque flowers
      purple presses   hard   rare larkspur pecks the ground alive

4. first-born is across the plain   near the pond, her dad
   his ears caught in complex frets   dreams   another

5. my daughter's face glistens   she's absorbed over water
   magic, magnetic   with toybox movement

6. she falls down   beside him, of him   but he's   already leaving
   I turn   scream   burst into   slow-motion running   it's freezing
   February   the plain rubble separates us

7. it's miles   axed out of time   before I pull her
   purple   before he returns from some encored reverie

   earthskin lies fallow   springtime's a lie

8. I hold   rock   de-cake her   of muck, mud   but   fear
   stains deep blackberry   it's one year before she permits
   bathing   sponge-baths rinse nothing clean

9. another steppe   years later   a different man stalks
   between children   cranes his head   useless at rearing
   transplanted whoopers

10. second marriage shaky   and doomed   despite mountain
    hikes   August grass spiked with   paintbrush   lupine
    this family so fragile   it separates

11. meadows now   hold nothing but   memory   cracked earth
    and a girl   who swam like a pollywog   for a second
                                                    then aged

~Gail Waldstein

chasm

there are loves that slip
into you   second selves

burrow below   mind-skin
more intimate than   twined tongues

so sprung they will   never release
but you don't know that   then

you're alive   hunger sated for the now
hope for grace   or mercy

the mist   the bed
frigid   early one morning

euphoria and ordinary   cannot co-exist
you know that   yet, yearning

desire   deep and needful   clings
like an intestinal parasite

you didn't factor   fingertip hunger
the body's   voracious appetite

the insatiable craving   of lips
to still smell him on your skin

you   haunted, bereft   remain
                                    infested

~Gail Waldstein

Motherhood

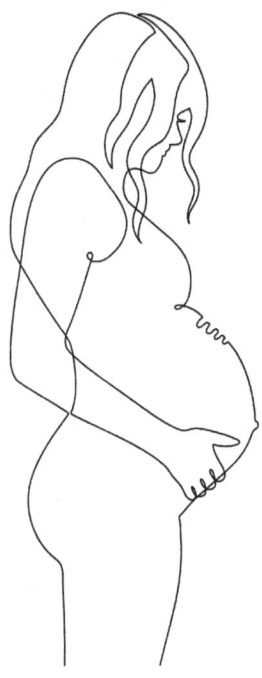

A Covid Mother's Day

In this
viral
ghost town
where
even the
ubiquitous
squirrels
at my
daughter's
nursing home
vanished
I stand
masked
beneath
her window
Hey, Sue!
Look
at the trees,
no squirrels!
and she
masked too
leans out
a floor up
They
must be
in prison
like me.
It's hard
to hear
her
soft sweet
voice
weak
with MS
I shout
Love you,
girl!
through my
N95
I can

barely
breathe
but we
chat a bit
& sing
"You Are
My Sunshine"
& try Yo-
Mama jokes
Yo Mama
so fat
she has
to wear
two masks
until
there is
nothing
more
to say
we wave
blow kisses
bye bye
I turn
to leave
walking
slowly
away
I can
hear
one tiny
bitter
wail
like
a squirrel
might make

~Petra Perkins

migration

    storks navigate
                        by magnetic fields
      genetic map

    follow their ancestral path
                        oceans and rivers

    fly thousands of miles

    rendezvous with their mates
    in their lifetime nest
          built on a chimney
                in a French village

          fairy tales   folk lore
    babies carried to their
    families   winged delivery

    no one knows   the story of your flight
    heavy with me
        your genes imprinted

    a piece of you

               left in another's nest

                      ~Brooke Granville

expression

        defined: *the process of making known one's thoughts or feelings*

she went home without me

        the unknown

                chased lonely

the secret

        circled

                an emptiness

her full breasts wept

        rings of truth

                ~Brooke Granville

no room

      your bedside in ICU
      flanked by your
            other daughter
                  your son

I   first born
                  given away

      wait
one state from you

          when I hear
grief sits with me

~Brooke Granville

in Big Sky

my birth mother built her home on Two Moons Road
shadowed by lone mountain

her second and third children
invited me
                after our mother died

to visit her lofted log cabin
        old upright piano as you walk in

her pen and ink drawing of a chief framed

kitchen filled with her sister's pottery
        large and small earth tone bowls

her jade tree   as old as the one in the house
I grew up in   with the mother who raised me

my two moons

                              ~Brooke Granville

new year's eve '88

seven and half pounds of you
home from the hospital

intimate strangers
we shared this body of mine
       yesterday

both of us hormone laced
milk yet to come

fatigue wrestles with adrenaline

pace   rock   cry
engorged breasts defy us

the ball drops

peel off our clothes
chest to chest   your cheek   my neck
       quiet

~Brooke Granville

passage

luminosity silhouettes her
darkness clasps the still form
as it glides from its lagoon
one final push   her mother bears down
face contorts
she grunts   panting in staccato
a head crowns   black hair emerges
pasted down atop a molded caput
until yesterday folded
in superb flexion   wedged against
pubic bone   tensed hinge ready
to spring   and then

cranial bones slide over one
another in silent overlap
eyelids wrinkle   two walnuts
tightly closed   wrappings slip
off this rumpled gift
unveil her long-awaited surprise
breathtaking   perfect
breath scratches   catches
hold   life ignites into flesh
air sacs expand like bubbles
echoes of her labor
they rest   spent
infant along her mother's torso
heart-tone soothing heart-tone
infant sucks
her mother's womb contracts
in remembrance

~Constance E. Boyle

colt

she prances in tall grass
beyond the house
circles the evening shadows   distorts
them in her frenzy   a vigorous nod—
mane flies from her neck
this filly stands five hands high
she skids to a stop   eyes widen

hooves   rake ground   kick
up brown clouds
                        she charges

Mom, you're home
we lock smiles   hers, so lustrous
I lose myself

~*Constance E. Boyle*

mom, you'll love this

my son and I inch up the Vegas coaster
dismissing
        do not ride if you
        have back or nervous conditions

strapped into the car   my hands grip
the side bars
        we near the top

this ride, his marriage
tomorrow merge and roar

around the edge into a voluminous loop

I shut my eyes against the drop,
the upside-down   hold

my breath   we hurtle   plummet
curve   *scream*
my son says and I do, a long, excited one

push-pulled
we laugh   shout   breathe

I love this son   this roller coaster, too

                  ~Constance E. Boyle

gravity slack belly

I suck in cold July air
bitter with pine
I crave the grasp of baby hand
around my now gnarled finger
I still twirl her ginger curl
across   cradle capped skull
my expired motherhood
my ticket to humanity
three times punched
is over   I'm being thrown
off the moving bus
onto macadam
my beating womb
labors to fill again
aches with futility

I long to re-plug
the bloody umbilical cord
I sleep   feign health
a fetal foot stirs
abdominal memories
mimes the flesh-mind
what it's like
at full term
I sicken it cannot come again
the coming of milk-time

~Gail Waldstein

womb-dreams

herds of horses   gallop
muscles move as if   in saddle

neurons record   the ride
or maybe   wire for the future

every emotion   sculpts his face
first days after birth

eyes drift   open   close
into the sky of   before

laughter   then   a grimace
forehead knots   to frown

a universe of passion   passes
mouth sucks   toes curl in milk ecstasy

precious son   of my daughter
carried by a   surrogate

his face shadows sorrow   blooms to joy
astride his horse   grasping the mane

yippee ki yay   to generous womb
beloved baby   who almost
                        wasn't

~Gail Waldstein

grief canal

in a hard household
sorrow gestates long

the way I sat   ready to go
my daughters packed   husband

absorbed   in his guitar   medical papers
the acne on his back

their brother already   brooding
inside me

the way I didn't leave then
gave birth again

Sarah's finch   *Spangle*
spackle-feathered jewel

died a year before   she'd taken
it in   all ordinary

until one night   nursing the baby
reading to her   *Spangle's gone*

tears   she
runnels into   me

~Gail Waldstein

and the sins

I keep the eight by ten   matte finish
in the family album   taken long before
you could walk   crocheted cap Nana made
covers your ears   ponderosa behind
your father   holding you high
you're grinning full   into the lens
which profiles him   proud smile

before he vanishes   and home upends
before guitar silence   spirals my laughter
to puce   before I return
folded   weeping   drugged
from the hospital   tongue stuck hard to
palate   arms released   from straight jacket
all movement stuttered

                                    I stop
at an accident one night   red lights spin
offer help   you're along   excited
although   he's gone   your dad   for years
I tell you how we met   almost your age
in med school   how he wanted to be a shrink
heal his father   make him laugh again
how I didn't want him   leached of empathy
how selfish I was

how you're to be a doctor   now
because no other child will
you'll have a common tongue
with your dad

how later pictures of you
in the album   are full-family
hippie groupings   seizing that
frozen moment   when we still knew
the fragrance of marijuana
the greedy jungle of desire

~Gail Waldstein

a vase of lonely

my daughter says
empty vases   are sad
mouths howling
for food or love or   maybe
I make that part up   we walk through
her Paris basement   where the
shelves home   excess bottles
boxed glass marbles   to fix stems

her lover buys her flowers, often
I do too   when I visit   it's Paris
vendors adorn corner pockets
even in January's freeze
when she calls   homesick   I fly over
retired now   and she asks so little
then   works through my visit

I spend days   honing ways   to close in
on her again   like we fell together weekends
she in Illinois   I, Ohio doctor
she   growing to prime   I, seeping from mine
we climb stairs   pass a forest of vases
she whispers   *empty, waiting*
and I think—in a flash—when she was five

drew a nurse   big kindergarten drawing
what I'll be   when I grow up
why nurse? I asked   *so I can come home*
and be with my children   I saw then
how hollow a cavity   I'd given her
called it childhood   called it love

~Gail Waldstein

Resilience

I'll tell you bipolar

the day she thought
she would fly
out the top of her head
and her body burst
trillions
of atoms exploding
her thorax, abdomen
arches and palms
electric with showers   a symphony
                        rapidly flat
of exhilaration   then   crescendos
                     overtaking
decrescendos
    over
                and over   LARGER
than she   until
she wanted diminuendo
needed it to end
unbearable   so exquisite
she couldn't

                               ~Constance E. Boyle

bipolar II

every 2 days I run
to the grocery—
toss berries   black/red /blue/
zucchini/more
garlic   a tubful of spinach/Swiss chard
in my cart   sacks of peaches from summer
192 ounces of olive oil
make dates
I can't keep   appointments
overlap   blast *O sole mio* on the player
drive 80 mph in a 55—
          stopped   I don't get a ticket

I rewind   play the Italian
song 10… 15 times

bi-polar   it's back
from a memory I can't bare   but do
                    awake
all night   conversations whir
in my head higher and higher   transcending

today on the phone speeding
through words   a friend hears me
laugh   long
blackboard scratches

I hang up   calm down   notice
how I blurted   grandstanding
soloist   drowning the tenor

                    ~Constance E. Boyle

the sun's claim

roof patio, southern Spain
   lavender skies   a generous
                                     stain of cerise...
I thought I missed the sunrise
forgetting it comes
after the sky colors

a shard flashes through a cloud
   ascending quickly   brilliance infuses
   being   you want to soar
   dazzled by the sun   moving
   through you this moment—

light secures you to the earth

~Constance E. Boyle

this time of Covid-19

    1.
which slip of paper will you draw?
a long remnant?
a short piece?
will the end be gentle   light rain
misting your body?
a torrent?   drowning organs   limbs
and face   in this time of Covid-19
a viral volcano erupts
abruptly   torches lives   covers
people in ash

    2.
ten days of cough   chills   fatigue
symptoms come in waves
no one   visits   we stay home
friends phone   family FaceTimes
Zoom classes
online concerts: Bocelli, Mary Chapin
Carpenter on guitar
time for yoga   reflection
on my life   before

    I read Nabokov's *Speak, Memory*
Leve's *An Abbreviated Life*
Marie Cardinal's *The Words to Say It*
                      work my memoir
breathe deeper   take in/ release
emotion / pain   then / now

    people of color   in poverty
stricken often   die often
this pandemic reflects inequity

    3.
Presume it's Covid my doctor says,

    delivery men in masks and gloves carry
groceries in   amid a baking powder shortage
after isolation   my husband and I walk

the block   admire the crocuses   jonquils

   rig cloth masks, secure with rubber bands
over ears

   one day   our Denver son, granddaughter
unseen for a month
stand ten feet away
lay masks they've sewn
on stone steps   pleated masks
with cloth ties
               we breathe easier

   4.
June 2020: our daughter, son-in-law, granddaughter
fly from Maryland to Colorado
to start their month stay   we visit   masked
bearing blueberries   cherries and bagels
meet on the porch of their Airbnb
my husband and I
on one side   they, on the other
cool breezes blow through   no hugs
no indoor visits   and yet   we're together

   we hope Covid won't linger

   5.
each day   the news is grimmer
worsening   as businesses reopen
should schools reopen this fall?
scientists ponder whether social distancing
more problematic
than disease for children

   Black Lives Matter   takes on import
our family embraces the movement   the fear
historic statues of inequality fall
inhumanity   inequality in health   still prevail

   6.
our ten-year-old granddaughter from Maryland:
brown eyes swim with love   music spills
through her mask   we play war

she turns over the winning card   dances
in joy   splays her arms
black braids jounce
I share her excitement and triumph

    and think back to the year I play games
most of summer
during a visit to my grandmother out west
I delight in marathons of *Canasta*
her peach cobbler cools on the counter

    today I carry zucchini bread from my kitchen
my granddaughter and I eat at a table in the condo lobby
mask as we swallow the last bite
I love your bread she says   *and playing cards*
                                                with you

    7.
which slip of paper will you draw

~Constance E. Boyle

East River moon

rides waves   my daughter and I bus down the FDR

my mind curls back   to when she was three   wrenched from me
on that other full-moon night   I was committed to   Payne Whitney
upper East-side nuthouse   elegant   linen tablecloths
silver-plate   clean, fresh   straightjackets

> *straightjacket: canvas garment with extra long sleeves, crossed over heart   tied in back; used 1770s through 20th century to restrain mentally ill; considered more humane than chains, rope*

forty years ago   labeled paranoid schizophrenic   Thorazine silenced
mind empty as the moon   I watched river reflect   moons   waltz the sky
through barred windows   drugs swelled me, dulled me   terrible tremors

> *swell: become rounder...bloat...slow movement of sea waves...do not break*

I broke   incarcerated   by my husband, her dad
love   laughter   trust   eviscerated   *my* M.D. irrelevant
injections   animal screams all night   constant threat: shock therapy

> *shock therapy: electroconvulsive treatment for mental illness begun 1938; electrodes on patient's head induce seizures, confusion, memory loss, cognitive impairment*

I still hear voices   soft, intermittent now   and when they come, they
erase decades of psychiatrists   along with   my carefully constructed self

> *schizo: split, from Greek; phrenia: mind, from Greek; current definition: long-term mental disorder; breakdown between thought, emotion, behavior...mental fragmentation*

my daughter thinks I should   forget   forgive   it's old history
and yet, and yet   my husband, love of my life   *put me away*

my children   career   life   stopped

I gaze at the river-moon   stunned by complexity of the mind
and time's
                                          viscosity

~Gail Waldstein

In the Closet

I can hear him   coming for me
it's that time   late evening
he wakes   after an hour or two
passed out   from drinking
vodka/gin/wine
a beer thrown in at lunch

I'm hiding   upstairs in the walk-in
now a hide-in
it's dark   behind boxes & coats
he'll never find me   he won't look
here   How long will I stay?

Two hours once   drenched in
hot summer sweat   lying on
soft sweaters   they smelled of
better times   & leather from
our old boots   they hiked
many mountains together

now   me   mature woman
hiding again   from a man
a man I seem to love   more
than myself

him   a really nice guy   a
prince of a guy   when he
isn't   "under the influence"   no
one would believe this   I must not
believe it   I knew   of course
I knew   about his weakness for
booze when we married   I
drank with him most evenings   but
what I did not know: how it was a
disease
did not believe it my   true mortal

enemy
an   insidious   hateful   cruel
nemesis
that would prove
I had no limits   no intolerance for
craziness

He is bellowing now   as he
stomps through every room
kitchen bedrooms basement office
garage   he sees my car
he goes outside   comes back in
"Where the hell are you, honey?"
he's at the closet door
he flings it open
he only calls me 'honey' when
drunk
I am shaking   I hold tight
Don't move
he's never hit me with anything but
words   which hurt as much as a
fist might   when he barrages
me with insults   in his blackouts
does not know   what he says
what he does   a madman

he moves on to the bathroom
I exhale
I decide finally   to leave
the closet   tiptoeing
on a path of eggshells
toward the inevitable argument

Next morning it will be
as if
nothing happened
Mr. Nice Guy
Mrs. Nice Guy

We play the addiction game
the co-dependent game
nine more years   before
sobriety wins

but first I haul the boxes &
boots   sweaters &
coats   everything that is mine
including all my fears
out of the closet

~Petra Perkins

my son's chair

leggy white petunias
grow through cracks
of our flagstone patio

three wrought iron chairs
around the table

the chair you moved last week
in overgrown grass
to face the sun

shirt off, sunglasses on
white cat figure-eights
your bare legs

the day of your wake
the sun finds your chair
cat at my feet

tomorrow
I will carry your chair
back to the circle

~Brooke Granville

Death/Grief

missing

not until   your suicide
    did they speak
words   withheld

we did it to protect you

didn't tell me   you were   bullied
    at school   beaten by your dad when staying with him

you   hugging me from behind while I washed dishes
    bringing me tulips on my birthday   the child with hair like mine
      you had a gun

you didn't tell me   no one told me   I didn't see

it was life-threatening

~Brooke Granville

the oh of suicide

not the sympathetic   oh
of accident   or elder's death

not the   oh   dropped voice
constant note

but sliding down the tongue
circled lips   trumpet of pity

his car   running in the garage
your body   broken by cement
her handgun   in the tub

the   oh   no

~Brooke Granville

I didn't dust for a decade

    when the feather duster
               came to the photograph
           I cried

    your four-year-old self
        red shorts
        striped tee
        grinning and running
        to me
    tennis ball in one hand

    blond hair   like a dandelion tuft
                  lifted in the breeze

~Brooke Granville

grief is nocturnal

patient   idles in the periphery
         of daily motion
occasional nod   or knock the wind from you
         daylight visit

     no

grief relishes darkness   alone time

to lie beside you
         whisper

just for you   replays   that scene
    over   and over   and over
      the what ifs   ricochet

       eventual

dreams sketch themselves   into nightmares

              ~Brooke Granville

listening for the dead

white marble hush
        I search the mausoleum
for my dead brothers
        Skipper and Buddy
                always five and seven

walking the neighborhood
        winter solstice
                sun   low

car struck them

their ghosts   young   impatient
        a fixture in our household

our mother afraid to love again

                      ~*Brooke Granville*

prayer for the light baby

my Pilates teacher says   *think*
of sleeping babies, how heavy they feel
dead weight   *tense those gluts, pecs,*
abs   *make them work*   I squeeze even eyelids
tight   see light babies   years of pathology
when I did post mortems   bad days up to
five   my breath draws her instructions in

the awake baby is light   I remember mine
writhing   squirming   seeking to get down
keep those butts up   she shouts
the heft of them from the car   late nights
how easy in morning   arms stretching up
from the crib   *they weigh less*   and I believe her
as if it's true, verifiable

all those autopsies   you'd pace yourself
because the morgue was   hot   or cold
your bent back strained   into preemie cavities
tiny torsos flexed   no rigor mortis
muscle mass too small to stiffen

you need breaks   to keep records straight
hair texture and pattern on scalp   ear anatomy
skin hydration   you need time   to summarize
charts, call clinicians   *keep going*   *engage every muscle*

weigh   each organ, take tissues and blood for
cultures   chromosomes   photograph malformations
major   and minor   preliminary diagnoses scribed
as if a baby could be   cubby-holed
                                          lift she drones

you and the secretary trade   you skim   next chart
the day thins   the morgue's clean   clorox on steel
another naked body   too little food, too much coffee
your hands tremble   *belly to spine*   *pull in with exhale*
exertion shakes you   like the bone-saw vibrates
tiny vertebral columns

sterility cloaks the room

like an infection

I'm exhausted   my children's dinner late
it's en-block evisceration   the very word   curdles
refrigerate organs   release body to mortuary
curl   tighter, harder   by morning   *you'll refresh*
formaldehyde chews nasal nerves   like leprosy
all meals tasting tin   even your baby's powdery
bottom tainted   till midweek

sorrow seeps through gloves

until   one Saturday night   around eleven
grandparents   from Wyoming   want to hold
their son's newborn, want to touch   baby flesh

in the morgue   you place   fresh cotton batting
in the skull   clean white pads in chest and abdomen
weeping, blood-soaked cloth removed
no baseball quick-stitch   in black cord tonight
fine catgut   hair wet-combed over   scalp seams
limp arms pushed through   kimono

she's inactive   in her pink blanket
and you think   how to explain   lightness
to these ranchers
    why   *she's feathery as down*

~Gail Waldstein

water baby

>Ridge Home, Denver, 1969

her head takes
three beds
body folds   sideways
tiny toddler size
only   she's eleven
contractures   secure her
as if she were a   pinned insect
on corkboard   awaiting study
feeding tube   intermittent nursing
sops her drool, soil   and the catheter

skin translucent beyond   porcelain
shadow features: nose, brows, slim smile   you
almost imagined   you want to think
ideas float behind sunset eyes
roaming walls   pupils rolled far down
the eyes are only white

her rind of cortex thins
despite shunts, failed shunts, replacement
stents   hemispheres almost collapsed
you stroke her forehead
watch for a reflex   any reaction   then
touch your growing belly
                            pray

~Gail Waldstein

second cancer

everything diminishes

lost are   lovers   the bling of love
husbands gone   passion deflates
the very body   alien   in a hospital bed

alarms clamor   lungs suck oxygen
all I do   for three weeks   is whisper
P-E-A-C-E   inside my fogged-head

unlike the time of Nam   back then
marching   young   fierce with life
and children   who now swarm bedside

solemn, scared   begging
remember how you love   us
think how you love our children

they chorus   choke on   *we love you Ma*
don't give up
I'm drowning   shriveled, shiver

get IV feeds   indwelling bladder catheter
colostomy fills, bursts   again and again
covered in shit

do I even want to live   *peace*   ricochets   in my skull
even flowers wilt   I try to say   *I love you*
lips part   I stutter   fall silent

I don't know how   I start to come
                              back to them

~Gail Waldstein

rapid

silk light slants   over mauve granite
in this grand expanse of canyon

stone   groaning   hot   a desert weight
like the young   mother
dead   at twenty-one

I autopsied her   years ago
closeted in the   old basement morgue
head and foot   at bitter ends of table

one leg half gone   cancer
I made that   diagnosis   took
stairs   two-at-a-time   from the OR

biopsy in hand   fleshy pink tissue
granular   with grey bone flecks   like mica in stone
hoped   bone wouldn't   nick the knife

of the microtome wheel   I spun
close to frozen block
cold as this river water   fifty degrees

air arcs to one-hundred twenty   in this
Arizona desert slices breath   like I sliced
eight micra sections

peeled tumor off   the blade with a
fine, sable brush   lifted each piece
delicate as lingerie

in pediatric pathology   the tint of tissue
is everything   pink normal   blue malignant
her slides   a blue wash

dense populations   exploded
                              osteosarcoma

in the canyon   black *Vishnu schist*
rivulets up   from earth-core   like a

slippery dark umbilicus
or the ropes which cord rafts   each night
against river   waves
days blend around bends   below beveled
ledges   sandstone   *Zoroastrian granite*
Angelbrite shale   names sage-scented

her knee pain
danced dreams   for weeks
stopped soccer practice   two months

then   doctors   x-rays
        amputation at
sixteen, sweetgod

wheel chair   prosthesis   grief

at the tongue of each rapid   water speeds
oarsmen shout   stay down, hang on
I kneel   on two knees   grasp guy-rope

years after surgery
love   runnels her
marriage, a baby

radiance   like a resurrection
accompanies them to   check-ups
all clear   silence flows like

after the canyon wren's   decrescendo
breaking day   each morning
the baby   two, then three   husband solid

her igneous life   her life of
time   until one day   she
didn't feel well   no pain   not short of breath

five years back then   *was* cured
and all she was was   not feeling well

like day's   end   on the   river
the way sand gives way   beneath insteps
forces labored   breathing

like giving birth   or coming

her desire   an imperative
and   in fairness, more time with
her daughter
her eyes   glaze dull
at the word   *malignant*   radiologist
shows her   lungs   not laddered rib-rungs

but   galactic   explosions
white against black as   she becomes   blue

withdraws   to her   chest-cave
time   dwindles at   warp-speed
her disease   cascades

raw as the river   *won't hurt you*
oarsmen chant   *rapids spit you out*
ten seconds, max   even big holes

her sky   scream-blue

you float   past millennia of   stone
purple   rose   griege
beauty holds danger   oarsmen warn

it's rocks that drown you   yet you know
no one   drowns   in   stone
she does

her lungs   uncuttable   with your
Stryker saw   sudden water's
two stories high   a grade ten   rapid

your oarsman's   beside you   outside
the raft   you yank her back   in
we do not   breathe   water

we've lost that simplicity

the young mother   hungered
for air   for her child's hair
auburn, curling

like currents   when water
furls under, flows upstream   eddies

her tumors   grow   drugs futile as
oarsman's strength   in a   whirlpool
                     the mother's breath   a rasp

unfathomable   as   geologic time

our river time runs down   porta-potties fill
as her lungs
the way we let this canyon seduce us thinking

the ride is all   the water   its rhythm
the world outside   unchanged
like her   laying her child   down

that last time   the horror   of that
                                 long embrace

wheezing   fighting   until she came
to me   that hot August
chest locked in tumors   hard as

riverwalls   I opened her
young then   climbed   the morgue table
wrestled stone-lungs   up

as if   to free
                her heart

~*Gail Waldstein*

two thousand miles

in sunrise I pass blue ducks
on a blue lake

drive to the Denver airport
the city looks blue

navy skyscrapers   faceless blocks on stilts
indigo against pewter clouds

                                days later
I leave
the Hudson   across from the city of dreams

from the plane window   a fogged-in sky
New York skyline   not quite—

ghost structures white
upon a whiter background

the buildings   figures, small
sailboats in a foaming sea

slide from view
just so   aging parents gray

drift
            to white

~Constance E. Boyle

a hike to a waterfall in Ithaca four weeks after

1)
I trample hundreds—
red   saffron   ocher

the path   shiny
with rain   leaves   layer thick

oak   maple   sumac
trickle down from branches

I retrieve
vibrant ones   stack on my palm

smoothe   guard   sprinkle
with water until I can pack them

I push towards the top   breathe
fast and shallow

2)
four weeks ago mother
struggles for breath

3)
I can't see who she is

memories rush like mercury
forward   back

silver flashes up/down the column

is she 7   87 or 3
newborn   just married

4)
at home I lift
out leaves   thin as paper

edges fold in at my touch
some break down like limbs

not even water restores

5)
denim hue suffuses
her face

she gasps five more times
after her heart stops

curls into herself   her face
leaves   regret

fear   grief
I can't ask which

6)
in the end
the whole leaf
                                stills

~Constance E. Boyle

Five Weeks

Holiday grief sucks more, it's
 rougher
Thanksgiving Day is the start of
 bleaker
December bloodshed is brighter and
 redder
Loved ones gone are somehow
 deader
December wallets spill out much
 greener
Buy Buy Buy will make you
 better
December food is thicker and
 sweeter
It stuffs the holes, makes hearts
 air-tighter
December spirits, one drink then
 another
Stay ahead of the pain, it may help
 smother
December nights, colder and
 lonelier
January 1st won't make you brand
 newer
Holiday grief, such a gut-wrenching
 matter

~Petra Perkins

Here and Away

In a box were locks of your black hair/ still shiny/ pressed flat by a physics book
I'd gently cut them/ bushy thick/ from your freckled neck/ our early geek period

Shall I blast your hair into orbit/ a DNA sample for aliens/ UPS by space capsule?
Space is where you lived/ in that cosmic head of yours/ you were all about flight

You built airplanes/ before you died in one/ we built rockets/ I was your rocket girl
Remember nights on the lawn/ we lay dewy and cool/ searching stars for the red

Amazed that we could even see the Red Planet/ up to 1000 x farther than the Moon!
We planned our lives together/ lightyears ahead/ as if we owned time and space

Yes/ I'd send your locks flying/ around Mars/ if my rocket could escape gravity
Imagine it/ hear the engines/ feel the thrust/ scar the sky/ visions can be memories

Your eyes like falling star flashes/ electrifying the dark/ traveling 186K mi/sec
In physics nothing dies/ it changes form/ so maybe you're a quasar?/ Fuck mystery

Dear husband/ my energy must stay here/ on Earth/ grounded in the present
I'm sending your hair/ after this last caress/ Goodbye, hair/ fly away to the night

~Petra Perkins

Heat

Mr. Yamaguchi is not stopping
at the *kyoju* tree
with others who gather
under its graceful arms
a veil of cool air sweet
with roses and
himawahai
this August day on his
way to work
one last time before a train
takes him home
to rejoin wife and baby
(finally!)
all summer out of town
a young man's daydreams
happy now, soaring
he glances skyward
over tree line
at an airplane
as something drops
a silent flash
brighter than sun
a most beautiful
silver lightning bolt (?)
makes daylight
seem dim, blinding
unbearable whiteness
his ears buzz, a sonic boom
deafening blast
he dives into a ditch
waves of intense heat
clouds like kinetic red
blooms in a bouquet
pale yellow stem
every thing is…what?
what is happening?
can't hear
can't see
can't breathe
he can't breathe

can't breathe
everyone, everything blowing
blowing
blazing
burning
inferno black with fuzzy
choking ash
.
.
.
Mr. Yamaguchi crawls out
to firestorms, fireballs
streets of shattered glass
trees, houses vanished
lifeless bodies…
others shrieking…
living dead…
some dying in front of him
skin
hanging
in folds
they stagger
arms outstretched
faces contorted or gone
a sight
unspeakably, horridly
unimaginable
new to human eyes
that can still see
a collective wail of misery
new to human ears
that can still hear
he finds a crowded shelter
spends the sweltering
day and a night
burnt flesh, black rain
relentless thirst
no respite from agony
he leaves, *must* get to family
boards train to Nagasaki
(still running!)
Mr. Yamaguchi rests seated
the long ride home

people in shock, dazed
another passenger
a quiet, younger man
carries a covered bowl
holds it still and tight
on his lap
someone dares to ask
What is it?
the man begins to shake
he cannot contain himself
weeps
as he gently lifts the cover
"My wife's bones. I am taking
her back to her parents."
Mr. Yamaguchi cries
embracing his family
collapses in bed with fever
a night and a day
as Mrs. Yamaguchi bandages
his painful burns
he rises to return to his job
a marine engineer
in Nagasaki
though weak from
a strange sickness
where he tells his boss of
the horrors
but the boss does not believe
his stories
of any bombing
of Hiroshima
says Yamaguchi is faking
his injuries
to cover his missed
days of work
"No single bomb can destroy
an entire city!"
They argue and at that precise
moment they are hit
by a blast
another mushroom cloud looms
high over a city
yet again Mr. Yamaguchi

survives
again
he escapes and journeys
on paths strewn with dead
and the dying
some, his friends
he runs home to find family
alive (a miracle!)
alive because they'd luckily
been in a tunnel when the
bomb exploded
gone to buy burn ointment
they are uninjured, it seems,
until years later
each suffers cancer
from radiation
but Mr. Yamaguchi
the engineer who writes
poetry
lives to be old and wise
Tsutomu Yamaguchi admits
he had considered
"honor killing"
himself and his family
but believes his destiny is to
leave a timeless
message for the world:

Nuclear bombs and people
cannot co-exist
Nuclear war is assault
on human dignity
Nuclear destruction is
never-ending atrocity

.
.
.

Are we humans de-horrified?
so hot with nuclear threat
or lost in denial
that we are deaf
to Yamaguchi's lessons
to our self-annihilation?

~*Petra Perkins*

Retreating

we lie on beds of lava
in reverent silence
gather cavewomen spirits

far out in the high desert
with scorpions and snakes
deer   a dormant volcano

families   jobs   left behind
drive here on a hot fall day
to a waxing half-moon night

converge   an ancient tantric
fire ceremony
take turns throwing

sage   sandalwood   shouts
Swa-ha!   Swa-ha!
at wind-smeared flames

sleep   like the long dead
wake   by cool sunrise
walk   tight steps in a

labyrinth   where natives
trod   tribes ago
How can I believe

I alone am   tormented?
every soul here   is
wild   with grief

~Petra Perkins

Grief Takes No Prisoners

At night he holds your hand if
the TV news
gets too scary. He holds longer
tighter
on 9/11 and during Covid and
shootings

Days are predictably regular:
read and write
chat and spat
soup & salad or carryout
nothing spectacular
Fall days he feeds sparrows
and squirrels
in the last golden hours 'til
dead of winter
You don't grasp the concept
of "the last"

Memory blurs yesterday into
the day before, or
tomorrow
You don't reckon the future of
certain moments...
the last kiss, the last time you
will touch
his silver hair, ever the mane
that stirred
a bit of leonine lust when first
you stroked it
You should laugh extra loud at
his last joke
or say of the last fiery sunset
"Hurry, come see!"
The last meal must surely be
grilled ribeye basted
in garlic butter
You could offer a last taste
of Bordeaux
though he tee-totaled, years

ago, when you
said you'd leave
He says you saved his life

You find him on the floor
eyes open, vacant
his breath stopped by... what?
whatever causes
stillness of stars
You don't get to memorialize
last pleasures
It is sorrowfully, irrevocably
too late

Grief presses a dead weight
on your life
until it dies, that life you led
for decades
You do still breathe and exist
in shockwaves
pushed to a new life without
critical parts
snatched from the clutch of
embrace
like clasped fingers grown
together
now torn asunder
nerves frayed and raw from
being ripped
Sometimes you must restart
more than once
and people often say "He is
still with you;
our loved ones are with us."

But you wonder about that
in the dark
when you are alone and the
silence smothers
and you can't text anyone after
midnight
even though people say "Call if
you need me

anytime."
You know you can't really
call them
at 3:00 a.m. when you're teary
cannot breathe
cursing heaven's decree
You die again and again, each
time you re-realize
the finalities of your old life

Your last exhale is not of your
human body
it's your pain body, the one that
succumbs
to grief

You begin again somehow
slant insight
with a larger heart that's been
to hell and back
stronger, deeper, tenderer.
Whoever
ventures among the cracks
lucky
to be there, to help you find
new "first times"
and you *will* remember the
last times
because they are with you still

~*Petra Perkins*

Spirit

aurora

> *rising light of morning...*
> *boreal is the north wind*
> *OED definitions*

1) imperative

diagnosis   macular   degeneration
I may not see   my children's faces
again   only feel   grandchildren grow

didn't think these thoughts   initially
didn't weep about   not reading

am I too old to learn   braille
what about foreign films   and
driving   can I live alone

> *macula   center of retina*
> *disease   blinds here first*
> *clotted blackness   gray shadows*

seized by a singular desire   I must
see the aurora   before sight's gone

I study these mysterious lights   a complex physics
solar eruptions   excite electrons   in our atmosphere
around both poles   produce

vivid   dancing   curtains of color

> *interstellar winds whip electrons*
> *toward earth at the speed of light*
> *186,000 miles/second*

big black blocks blot   my sight   too soon
my daughter says   *I want to take you to see*
the northern lights   *soon*   touched I say

let's wait and see   *no* she insists   *now*
while you're able

> *when I had physics matter was solid,*
> *liquid, gas   now there's plasma:*
> *an ionic state   99% of visible universe*

2) Iceland

black midnight sky   earth below is   white
the sea white   the edge of everywhere   burns white
the world so white you see   silence

people here are pale too   women's hair so fine
it holds no pigment   gleams in moonlight

my elder daughter joins us   it's January
we tour   four stingy hours of daylight
the earth's   tectonic plates scored with

black lava crevices   geysers   volcanoes
bubbling pots   sulfur-fumed air
tundra cracked by a   crenulated black rift

guide points   *the plates*   strain apart   there
the cold land imitates   our unease   childhoods
gone, along with laughter   three of us awkward

green moss everywhere   large gray lake   mars
a greige plane   near ancient ruins   Þingvellir

                   planet's first parliament   930 A.D.
                   settlers assembled each June
                   law-speaker recited codes

my daughters say little   of their private lives
polite opinions only   emotions concealed
do they fear   my old   megaphone authority

do they hoard secrets   to feel safe   they care for me
offer an arm to cross streets   where light is dim
I hate this new frailty   struggle to keep up

so much ice   the week ticks by   we relax
into our   isolations

3) night sightings

ride from Reykjavik   and light pollution

a hillside   an inverted blue-black bowl
suspends stars cocoons us   we lean back

pink clouds fur the horizon   shape-shift   block
the moon   the milky way   amorphous ether
is this it

then   a pale spring-green streaks
fantasias   dance   whirl   dizzying

we crane necks like   wild white swans
it's frigid   but our eyes stay wide
smiles swirl to laughter   a miracle

guide says
> *the sun's plasma spirals*
> *through space   creates magnetic fields*
> *which intersect with earth's poles*

the green abates   another locale   no doubt here
viridescent shapes   traffic the sky

second night   distant mountain   bursts of
green spear horizon   twist and   pulse
last spot   a lighthouse   at peninsula's end

coldest wind   wild waves   breaks against seawall
crescent moon rides the ocean   we inhale salt mist

great green scythes   gash the sky   ellipses form
around each other   like a mother clasps her child
emerald drapery   explodes   indelible

we're in a kind of rapture   guide serves cookies cocoa
      the sky exhausts itself

> *aurora colors: oxygen in stratosphere*
> *emits green light   at low altitudes it's red*
> *nitrogen vibrates purple, pink*

grateful for my daughters'   generosity
their gifts of time   this week together   brooks distance
we blink apart again   store retinal
                                incandescence

~Gail Waldstein

flying

1) *making flight or passing through the air*
2) *floating, fluttering, waving, hanging or moving freely in the air (flying banners, flying hair)*
3) *moving swiftly, which she was, by her own volition, she wanted to see everything there was to see*

Visiting her daughters, young women, one in class, the other with friends. The mother has an afternoon. She loves flying to this city, infrequent, she lives across the country. The night before, the three women dined at an Upper East Side restaurant, later, they sipped mojitos with lots of mint on the 12th floor of her hotel. Windowed on three sides, the lovely bar ran the length of the hotel. Overlooking the 59th Street Bridge, lit with lights.

White

absence of	*filled with*
berries	*roses*
invite	*death*
helicopters	*circles*
unfulfilled	*unfilled*
textured paper	*moonlight walks*

She strolls rose gardens, tight blooms barely open, petals soft, centers of rich perfume. Loves the coast, waves breaking hard near her body as she sits on the wet shore. Reads Neruda late at night, awake past midnight.

Dark coffee from Kenya delights her, especially in intriguing cities, local cafes. And philosophizing. Sipping Merlot infused with cherries. She likes to pass through revolving doors. Dark chocolate undoes her. Fill the tub with bitter chocolate. More than a few almonds. She loves and dislikes flying. Take-offs, landings, fast, hard, out-of-control. Sound of wheels, incline/angle of departure. Then, the let-down. Her return.

White

cumulous clouds	*strings, sails*
parachutes	*silk*
life	*ghosted*
happiness	*chalk*
wedding gown	*veiled song*
washed fences	*epiphany*
in terror	*no trespassing*

A downpour of flakes fall like miniature parasols. Heavy snow in Manhattan. Late January. She walks blocks, 30, 40, past two-story brownstones with black iron fences. Despite the approach of evening, snow lightens everything, she is flying into white. Doorways darken, but she's warm, in love with the world, alone but not alone. Light suspends time.

~Constance E. Boyle

Beehive mountain

on shaded edge of
a wild flowered meadow

we drop to the ground
strawberries

       ripe

generations of my
newly found family

picking   eating
tiny red berries

the freshness of it

~Brooke Granville

Waxing Crescent

    Hectic holidays   driving home spent   intent
going the devil on ice   everyone belted   sleeping fast
  my routine side glance ->   the moon, a surprise

        In the low southwestern sky
   where dusk leavened our winter evening
  he peered   a tipsy night-watch   or savvy spy
     a wise-guy appearing to mock me
as I sped by with the blaze of reckless shooting stars

  He lingered over distant craggy mountaintops
       black stains looming in heaven
       then slid down to touch a tip
     shining a dazzle-white sliver grin
       keeping his Venus eye on me

    I stopped the car at his insistence
    time idled   a minute   maybe three
     he cast one wry Cheshire smile
      upended in a sideways smirk
...now a jeer... next, a smudge into tight kiss-lips

... a comic vertical line... down to a sparkly dot...
   seconds before sinking into inkblot hills
  ... swallowed by dark... leaving a mirage

Just in case my awe waxed incomplete   he returned
  brazen on high-beam   between a two-peaked arc
         for his last quick twink

Everyone woke   in stark question-mark silence.
  I broke it to explain: "T'was Officer Moon
        who stopped our tracks
   for speeding   let us off with a warning –
                       this time."
   And this time they all but believed me
     loony

                                       ~Petra Perkins

Celestial

Waterfalls   it is said
are where angels live
practice their singing
compose heaven's music
ethereal tunes   sustained chords
shifting keys   major to minor
scores   with no discernible lyrics
soprano/tenor   reaching skyward
one long *AhhhHHHHHH*
alto/bass   dipping low
OHHhhhhhhhhh
you may hear them but
not loudest   in coldest weather
when they gather
folded wings   laced in ice
slowed by Winter's interlude
enchantingly
sowing eloquent praises
in trickling voice   echoes
softened by forest limbs
perhaps you see
glimmers of the chanters
in glacial shadow
when snowflakes spark
as if   fireflies
reflecting light off auroras
pinging   like star twinks
shooting moonbeams
making of them   lanterns
in the darkness of rocks
caverns   where waterfalls
stop falling   as they linger for rest
through longest night
past equinox
divining *hope* for the new year
waiting   anticipating
a ray of sun's warmth

In early Spring   bursting with song
the vigorous downbeat of a concerto
convenes its three-season rapture
melting angel hearts
you might marvel   how they
loosen the icicled cascades
their braided hair   silvery strands
among baubles of clinging frost
you whisper   possibly
but not for long   as the
sleeping falls awaken   perform
shy melodies   then more and
more   in harmony
come forth   tuning up
falling down   fast together
one after another
uniting into multitudes
alive with celestial rhapsodies
now bowing   flowing with abandon
flinging forward to greet
the lake   the river   the gully
where canyon animals scurry
as waterfall vapors   turn to hail
on dewy crisp mornings
angels open and stretch their wings
cracking ice   watch them soar
fly over cliffs   to nourish
sacred life below

Summer now glorious
their compositions gain
movement   volume   drama
you are drawn to the rhyme   to rhythm
pulsed by churning water   a magnetic force
beckons   come   *come*
you make the trek
unaware what shivers await
senses   stunned by nature's powerful
masterful   thunderful
artistry   a promise to enthrall
you will never forget   this moment
ionic freshness unleashed
Earth's frothy white blaze of tears

landscaped by the season's
deepest hues   curious bottomless pools
rainbow ribbons glow at waterfall's end
you spend an hour   or a day
arrive from far away
to hear the gush
inhale the mist
experience the surge
see cliffbirds dive
plunge like arrows from aloft
their luck guided by angels
it is said
you gaze above   into topless sky
above your secret place on earth
beyond vast mysterious realms
and you wonder how
they come suddenly into your space
cliffbirds   waterfalls   angels

One could say
only the luckiest of trekkers
bear witness
to angelic play in Autumn
as burnt-orange/crimson-purple things
mingle with water's journey
forge paths back into earth
from soil   to air   to angel dust
every waterfall
lavished upon mystical vistas
profound majesty
tinged golden by evening's slant of light
where   if you are spirit amongst them
you memorize the concerto
the bejeweled scenario
stash these
in the treasure chest
of your mind
to open on the longest
winter night
when you need solace
faith   magic
or
hope

~Petra Perkins

Through the Pane

"Reflection occurs when light moves from a medium
with one index of refraction into a second medium
with a different index of refraction."

    A beauty of this explanation
    is that *people*
           can be the medium
    When we focus the light of our eyes
            onto another   (or into another)
    reflection occurs

"Explore bending of light
between two media
with different indices of refraction.
See how   changing from   air
  to water
       to glass
alters   the bending angle?
    Play with
          prisms of different shapes and make rainbows."

We may have once seen a rainbow, discussed how it happened.
            You may have wanted to make a rainbow.
I may have said,
           You're spoiling the magic
(as if it were somehow less romantic
           to know how a rainbow happened).

Centuries ago,
French scientist-teacher-philosopher
Father of Analytic Geometry
René Descartes
(author of "Passion of the Soul")
made rainbows
for his beloved wife
… with one single drop of water.
(The rainbow ray is named in his honor.)

You may have persisted, persuaded:
"Notice that your rainbow is a special distribution of colors
whose reference point is your eyes; no one else will ever see it.
It is literally   uniquely   for your eyes only   when light enters."

Make this memory with me   you may have said   in your way.

Rainbow: an arch of colors formed   in the sky
    caused by refraction   and dispersion of Sun's light
by rain, or other water droplet in the atmosphere   (or tears)

I see you through the pane
                  bending my light toward you
shining all your hues
                  making reflections for me
to remember, forever

      you sail bejeweled waters,
                scale mountains until you become them
if I move slightly   I see you in altered light
                sharp here, smooth there, you
reflect even now, though far away
      you live in refractions of my memory
            where we made rainbows

How to Bend Light: *"Look at sunlight through c r y s t a l s*
    to enjoy colors.
There is an optimum angle to shine light through
    to get the biggest splitting of color vibrations.
    Try shining light at various angles, adjust it,
        and you will position spectrums at their best."
        -René Descartes (said, possibly, to his wife)

Yes, there you are in my looking glass:
    a sparkle on the ocean you sailed;
    a mountain shadow you climbed into;
    a glint on murky sky where your plane slipped into clouds.
In my mind's eye-light I see your rainbow
    bobbing red/yellow flags on blue seas,

an orange vest against green hills,
    the flying silver dot as it moves to black
forever invisible to indices of refraction, and to me............

B e n d your light to our memory. See our reflection
    playing   through my pane.

~Petra Perkins*

    *Dedicated to first husband, Terry,
    and son, Rod, who perished in an airplane

Credits and Acknowledgments

CONSTANCE E. BOYLE, M.F.A. resides in Denver, CO. For many years Connie worked as a physician assistant for Denver Health in pediatric and adolescent primary care. Her poetry book *Liberties* was published by Plan B Press in 2024. *Double Exposure* (poetry chapbook) placed first in the 2005 Plan B Press poetry competition. Her poem "flying" was second runner-up in the 2014 Faulkner-Wisdom Competition. Her poem "dance 101" won first place in the 2012 Colorado Authors League contest in the single poem category. Journal publications include *Dogwood, So to Speak, PMS, (poemmemoirstory)*, and *Sliver of Stone*. She has eleven poems in the anthology *la forza di vita: Caffeinated Poems* (ed. Roberts and Douglass, 2011). Currently, Connie is working on poetry, a memoir and short fiction. See https://coloradopoetscenter.org/poets/boyle-constance/ for more.

Grateful acknowledgment is made to the editors of the publications in which the following poems, some in slightly different forms, previously appeared.

- *Double Exposure*: "attic," "kayaking in a two-person boat," "stoop" and "two thousand miles"
- *Liberties*: "bipolar II," "dance 101," "flying," "I didn't know," "I'll tell you bipolar" and "in-house"
- *La forza di vita: Caffeinated Poems*: "dance 101"
- *PMS poemmemoirstory*: "bipolar II"
- *So to Speak*: "flying"
- *The Human Touch*: "a hike to a waterfall in Ithaca four weeks after" and "I'll tell you bipolar"

* * *

BROOKE GRANVILLE, a Denver native, has been writing poetry for fifty years about nature, family and relationships. An adoptee, she met her birth mother, which led to connecting with her two half-siblings, two aunts and twelve first cousins. She is writing her memoir on finding this family, the reactions and interactions of three generations on both sides of the story.

Brooke's poetry has appeared in the *Denver Post, Winter Park Manifest, Columbine Poets of Colorado, Buffalo Bones,* and *Refuse to Stay Silent*. She contributed poetry in a multimedia collaboration, *Umbered,* and has published three chapbooks, *Halfway, Collected,* and *Light Dust.*

* * *

PETRA PERKINS is a Colorado author of poetry, fiction, memoir, essay, humor, screen and stage play. After a 25-year career in aerospace engineering and management, she became immersed in more creative pursuits, especially writing. Petra's work is widely published, and has won awards in multiple genres, including the Faulkner-Wisdom Poetry Gold Medal and a Pushcart Prize nomination in Creative Nonfiction. See PetraPetra.com for more.

Grateful acknowledgment is made to the editors of these publications in which the following poems have appeared. Some have been lightly revised.

- *Art Ascent Magazine, Portrait Issue*: "The Kiss"
- *Blaze*: "Celestial"
- *DoubleDealer Magazine*: "Through the Pane"
- *Dreamquest*: "Waxing Crescent"
- *Elephant Journal*: "Heat"
- *Hippocampus Magazine*: "Here and Away" (formerly titled "Insight")

* * *

GAIL WALDSTEIN, M.D., was a pediatric pathologist for over 35 years, working at Children's Hospital, Denver most of that time. She also single-parented three children for fifteen of those years. She began creative writing in the late '90s, winning awards for fiction, creative non-fiction and poetry. Her work appears in *Nimrod, New Letters, Zone 3, The Iowa Review, Peal* and numerous other journals and anthologies. Two essays were nominated for Pushcarts. She received fellowships from Colorado Council for the Arts, Helene Wurlitzer Foundation and Rocky Mountain Women's Foundation. Two poetry chapbooks won prizes: *AfterImage* from Plan B Press in 2006, and *The Hauntings* from Swan Scythe (First Place) in 2014. A collection of essays and stories, *To Quit this Calling, Firsthand Tales of a Pediatric Panogist*, was a Bakeless finalist in 2005 and was published by Ghost Road Press in 2006. An essay, "Warehousing the Elderly" won first place in the Faulkner-Wisdom competition in 2024. See https://www.pw.org/directory/writers/gail-waldstein-md for more.

We gratefully acknowledge the following publications, in which the poems listed below have previously appeared, some in slightly different forms.

- *AfterImage*: "and the sins," "grief canal," "prayer for the light baby," "through meadows and marriages."
- *Harpur Palate*: "Prayer for the Light Baby"
- *Rock & Sling*: "water baby"
- *Seven Hills Review*: " a vase of lonely," "runnel" (retitled "chasm")
- *The Comstock Review*: "hymn"
- *The Double Dealer*: "rapid
- *The Hauntings*: "a duet of novices," "a vase of lonely," "Daddy," "helium," "hymn," "rapid," "runnel" (retitled "chasm"), "water baby"

www.ingramcontent.com/pod-product-compliance
Lightning Source LLC
Chambersburg PA
CBHW070147080526
44586CB00015B/1884